Wolf

in your
Kitchen

Contents

Written by Inbali Iserles

Collins

1 Good dog!

Humans and dogs go back a long way. Cats didn't enter our homes until 4,000 years ago. Horses were tamed 6,000 years ago. Even sheep – among the first **tame** animals – were wild until 10,000 years ago.

Dogs became our friends around *15,000 years ago*! They have lived beside us for so long, it's easy to forget that they were once wild.

What did the first dogs look like? Were they huge and shaggy, like deerhounds? Were they tiny with short fur, like Chihuahuas?

Were they fierce or friendly?

How did they come to live among people?

It's time to sniff out the answers to these questions! We are off in search of the first dogs.

Dogs come in all shapes and sizes.

deerhound

Chihuahua

3

What are dogs?

🐾 Dogs mostly eat meat, although they enjoy snacks like carrots and berries.

🐾 Dogs have an amazing sense of smell. They also have great eyesight and hearing.

🐾 They have been **bred** by humans for thousands of years.

🐾 Different types of dog are used by humans for **tasks** such as hunting, **herding** sheep, pulling sleds, protecting our homes, working as police dogs or guide dogs, or simply for friendship.

cocker spaniel

Chihuahua

What's different about dogs?

Cats and dogs are the most popular pets in the world. But while cats are all about the same size – usually between three kilograms to five kilograms – healthy adult dogs can weigh from 1 kilogram to over 110 kilograms!

Great Dane

rough collie

5

2 The perfect pooch

Types of dogs are called "breeds".
Popular breeds include beagles,
corgis and poodles. Look at
their ears and the shapes
of their faces.

Why are dogs so different
from each other?

Furry fact

There are around
350 breeds of dog.
No other tame animal
has as many varieties!

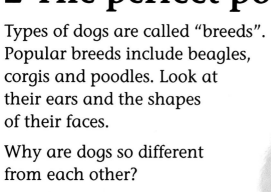

corgi

poodle

dachshund

"Sausage dogs" are good at getting into small places.

Breeds did not come about naturally. They are the result of careful efforts by humans to raise dogs that are better at particular tasks.

For example, dachshunds, also known as "sausage dogs", have very short legs. Over many years, humans bred dogs with short legs. From each **litter**, they picked the puppies with the shortest legs to breed again once they were old enough.

In the end, they were left with very short-legged dogs.

Hunting dogs

Why did humans try so hard to breed dogs with very short legs?

Because these plucky little pooches were good at chasing badgers into small tunnels.

Many dog breeds were used by humans for hunting.

Greyhounds were once royal hunting dogs. Their speed made them good at chasing animals like hares and deer.

Labradors are skilled at bringing things back to their owners. They were bred to fetch birds like ducks that had been shot by hunters.

Furry fact

Greyhounds are the fastest dog breed. They can run 72 kilometres per hour.

Terriers are usually small dogs. They were bred to hunt small animals. Jack Russells and Border terriers were used to chase foxes away from henhouses.

Border terrier

Not all breeds were traditionally used for hunting. How else have humans used dogs?

Herding dogs

Dogs like Border collies have been used as sheepdogs for thousands of years. These quick, clever dogs are easy to train and love to perform tasks for their owners.

Border collies need a lot of exercise.

Sled dogs

"Spitz" dogs include breeds that started in the far north, near the Arctic Circle. They have long coats, pointed ears, and tails that curve over their backs.

Spitz dogs, such as Samoyeds and Siberian huskies, were bred by **nomadic** people to pull sleds through the snow.

Huskies pull a sled in Lapland.

Furry fact

The word "spitz" means "pointed". Most spitz dogs have long, pointed **muzzles**.

New tricks

Some dogs that were once used for hunting or other tasks are now treated as family pets. Others are used for new tasks. For example, Labradors are popular guide dogs for blind people because they are easy to train and the right height to lead a human.

a Labrador guide dog

3 Old dogs

Wolves hunt as a pack.

We have looked at a few different types of dog.
We know that most dogs were bred to perform tasks.

But what did the first dog look like thousands of
years ago? And who were its **ancestors**?

Furry fact

Dogs have an incredible sense of smell. It is thought to be 10,000 to 100,000 times more powerful than ours!

To answer this question, let's look at the wild cousins of dogs. These are animals such as jackals, wolves, foxes and coyotes. Together with tame dogs, they all shared an ancestor 40 million years ago.

Dogs' wild cousins have a lot in common. They are **social**, preferring to live in family groups. Some hunt in **packs**.

What did the first dogs look like? At different times, scientists thought that tame dogs started off as one of these furry **suspects**. Who are dogs' earliest ancestors?

African wild dogs   foxes   wolves

What do you think? Which one looks most like modern dogs?

grey wolf   coyote   African wild dog

Furry fact

The smallest relatives of dogs are fennec foxes. They are no larger than kittens and weigh just one kilogram.

Furry fact

The largest relatives of dogs are grey wolves. They weigh up to 65 kilograms. Nose to tail, a wolf is the length of a tall human!

black-backed jackal

beagle

red fox

fennec fox

4 African wild dogs

African wild dogs have long legs, big ears and splodgy fur in patches of black, brown, white and yellow. They live in the woods and open **plains** of Africa.

They travel in large family groups that can number over 30 members! African wild dogs hunt as a pack and have one of the best success rates of any **predators** because members of the pack are so good at working together.

Like tame dogs, African wild dogs are social.

Furry fact

African wild dogs can reach
72 kilometres an hour at a run.
That's as fast as greyhounds,
the fastest tame dogs.

African wild dogs share a lot in common with tame dogs. They are social, clever animals that are excellent hunters. They are also the only one of our suspects with "dog" in the name! The first dogs must have been African wild dogs, right?

Furry fact

In a pack of African wild dogs, there is only one pair that has pups. The rest of the pack helps raise and look after the pups.

African wild dogs are certainly wild – but they aren't really dogs!

Wrong! Scientists checked the blood and bones of African wild dogs and discovered that they are not closely related to tame dogs. Unlike our own dogs, African wild dogs are happiest when left alone by humans.

5 Foxes

There are over 20 different types of fox. While some
like the fennec fox are smaller than cats,
most are somewhere between the size of a cat
and a cocker spaniel. All foxes have large ears shaped
like triangles, pointed snouts and long bushy tails.

grey fox

Furry fact

In Japanese traditional tales, foxes are magical! They are "**shape-shifters**", able to change into human form.

Red foxes

Red foxes are the most common type of fox.
They are found on every continent of the world
except Antarctica.

Compare the red fox with the shiba inu dog.
The shiba inu has a foxy face and thick ginger fur.
The two animals are even similar sizes.

shiba inu dog

red fox

Arctic foxes

The shiba inu is a type of spitz dog. So is the beautiful Japanese spitz.

Now look at these photos showing an arctic fox in its winter coat and a Japanese spitz dog.

Going by appearances, you might think that dogs are tame foxes. But is it true?

arctic fox

Japanese spitz

Looks can be deceiving!

Scientists used the **remains** of **ancient** wild members of the dog family to understand how these animals changed over millions of years. A very long time ago, dogs and foxes shared an ancestor. But ten million years ago, foxes started to develop differently to jackals, wolves, coyotes … and dogs!

jackals, wolves, coyotes and dogs

foxes

Furry fact

Foxes live in family groups called "skulks".

Scientists have discovered that *all* tame dogs – from Europe to Asia and Africa, through North to South America, and even in Australia – have the same wild ancestors. But they are *not* foxes.

the nine-tailed fox from Japanese traditional tales

6 Wolves

Wolves are dogs' largest cousins. They live in packs made up of family members.

Wolves were once found across the Northern Hemisphere, through North America, Europe and Asia. Sadly, wolf numbers have shrunk as human cities have taken over their wild lands.

Today, small numbers of wolves survive in Europe and America, with larger groups in cold and wild places like Canada and Russia where there are fewer people.

arctic wolves

Furry fact

Wolves are fantastic predators. They hunt as a team. This allows them to catch animals that are much larger than themselves, such as deer and elk.

Wolves are closely related to jackals and coyotes. But are they closely related to dogs?

Furry fact

When humans get hot, we sweat to lose heat. Dogs can only sweat through their paw pads, which doesn't lower their temperatures enough. This is why they **pant** through their mouths and noses. Panting helps them cool down by breathing out hot air and breathing in cold air.

Dogs pant to keep cool.

What do wolves and dogs have in common?

🐾 Both are social: they love company.

🐾 They use their ears, mouths, tails and voices to "talk" to each other.

🐾 They leave messages for each other by urinating!

🐾 They usually live for about 12 to 14 years (although wolves die younger in the wild).

🐾 They wag their tails when they are happy.

What are the differences between wolves and dogs?

🐾 Wolves have larger and stronger teeth than dogs.

🐾 Wolves are shy and avoid people. Dogs are usually bolder with humans.

🐾 Wolves are built for running and springing for hours. Most dogs tire more quickly.

🐾 Dogs can have puppies at different times of year. Wolves have pups just once a year.

🐾 A mother dog usually raises her puppies alone. Wolf packs raise the pups as a team.

Other differences between wolves and dogs

good at problem-solving alone

howls

smaller eyes

looks to humans to help solve problems

rounder skull

barks

wolf

dog

Did dogs come from wolves?

Scientists compared living dogs and wolves, along with ancient bones and remains. Early experiments seemed to show that dogs came from grey wolves, but we now know that this is not quite right.

A twist in the tail

Tests show that dogs and grey wolves share a common ancestor – a type of wolf that is now extinct.
Dogs and grey wolves probably developed as different animals at least 15,000 years ago. But some scientists think it may have happened as long ago as 40,000 years!

Grey wolves are closely related to dogs, but they are not their ancestors.

7 A place by the fire

Even if some wolves became dogs *only* 15,000 years ago, that is still a long time before humans settled down and began to grow crops or build towns.

15,000 years ago, humans hunted and found food, which they cooked over a fire. What made the wild, ferocious wolf creep out of the forest to sit by our firesides?

Scientists don't agree on how wolves were tamed. What do you think?

Here are some ideas:

🐾 It probably happened somewhere across the huge **landmass** of Asia and Europe.

🐾 Dogs could have been tamed more than once by different groups of people, making it harder to pinpoint a location.

🐾 Dogs may have bred with wild wolves after they were tamed!

Survival of the friendliest

Scientists used to think that humans stole wolf cubs to use for hunting. This seems unlikely. Wolves were tamed when humans were still nomadic. How can you tame wild pups when you are walking from place to place?

It's more likely that the friendliest wolves dared to come close to humans. Perhaps these wolves ate the humans' leftover food. Maybe they scared other predators away. Over time, social wolves moved their focus from a love of their pack to a love of humans.

That is when wolves became dogs.

Furry fact

When a dog gazes into its owner's eyes, something amazing happens. Both dog and human feel an emotion caused by a chemical in their blood. It's the same emotion that mother animals (including humans) feel when they see their babies!

8 The first dogs

We have seen the dramatic way that dog breeds differ from one another. We have found out the amazing truth that *every single dog* – from the tiny Chihuahua to the giant Great Dane – came from the same wolf ancestors.

But which breed of dog is most closely related to wolves?

GERMAN SHEPHERD?

POMERANIAN?

DOBERMANN?

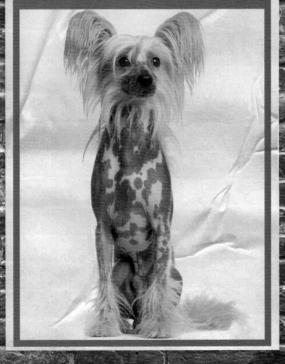

CHINESE CRESTED?

The secret of the spitz

Did you guess the German shepherd? These powerful working dogs have been bred for their **resilience** since the 19th century. Despite their wolfish looks, they are not as closely related to wolves as little Pomeranians!

Scientific experiments show us that spitz dogs such as the Alaskan malamute, the Siberian husky, the shiba inu, the Finnish, German and Japanese spitz, and even the Pomeranian, are the closest dogs to wolves, along with the basenji and Australian dingos!

Pomeranian

As the first wild animals ever tamed, dogs have come a long way. Their loyalty has moved from the pack to their human owners. We have bred dogs into the perfect hunters, herders, protectors and friends. As we have shaped the lives of dogs, they in turn have shaped our own.

Alaskan malamute

Finnish spitz dog

All these dogs are spitz dogs – the closest dogs to wolves!

Glossary

ancestors the members of a dog's (or human's) family that lived before it

ancient very old

bred have babies with

herding gathering together

landmass large area of land

litter a group of animals born to the same mother at the same time

muzzle nose and mouth

nomadic moving from place to place, bringing their home with them

packs groups

pant breathe quickly and loudly with your mouth open

plains wide, flat, open areas

predators animals that kill and eat other animals

remains an animal's (or human's) body after they have died

resilience ability to recover

shape-shifters creatures in stories that can change shape

social being around other animals or people

suspects people (or animals!) who may have done something

tame an animal that is not afraid of humans and is not dangerous

tasks jobs

Index

Where did dogs come from?

African wild dogs

- very social
- live and hunt as a pack
- spotted on the African plains

Foxes

- clever and gentle
- hunt alone (but live in family groups)
- found in every continent except Antarctica

Wolves

- closely related to jackals and coyotes
- live and hunt as a pack
- mostly found in cold climates

Ideas for reading

Written by Christine Whitney
Primary Literacy Consultant

Reading objectives:
- be introduced to non-fiction books that are structured in different ways
- listen to, discuss and express views about non-fiction
- retrieve and record information from non-fiction
- discuss and clarify the meanings of words

Spoken language objectives:
- participate in discussion
- speculate, hypothesise, imagine and explore ideas through talk
- ask relevant questions

Curriculum links: Science: Animals; Writing: Write for different purposes

Word count: 2554

Interest words: breed, herding, tasks, packs, tame

Resources: paper and pencils

Build a context for reading

- Ask the group if anyone has a pet dog or knows anyone who does. What breed of dog do they have? Ask for a volunteer to tell the group about a dog they know.
- Challenge the group to list the tasks dogs do for and with humans, for example a sheepdog *herds* sheep.
- Play 'five-in-three'. Challenge children to think of five facts about wolves and/or foxes in three minutes.
- Introduce the words *breed, herding, tasks, packs, tame*. Ask each child to suggest a sentence which uses one of these words correctly. Remind children to use the glossary to explain words they do not understand.

Understand and apply reading strategies

- Turn to the contents page and read through the different chapters in the book. Ask for volunteers to say which chapter they are most interested in reading and why.